MARTINE BELLEN

PLACES PEOPLE DARE NOT ENTER

MARTINE BELLEN

Potes & Poets Press, Elmwood, Connecticut • 1991

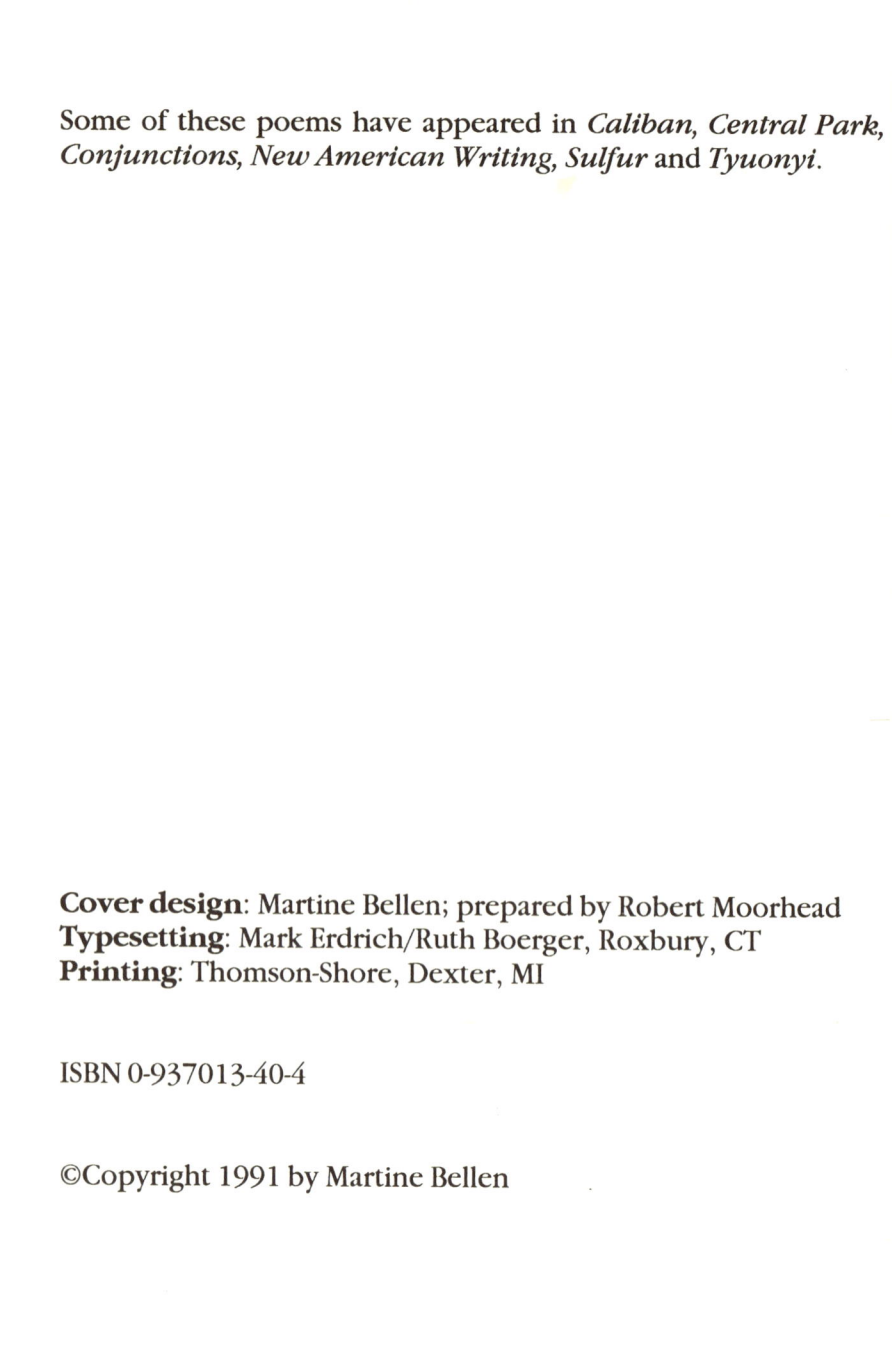

Some of these poems have appeared in *Caliban, Central Park, Conjunctions, New American Writing, Sulfur* and *Tyuonyi*.

Cover design: Martine Bellen; prepared by Robert Moorhead
Typesetting: Mark Erdrich/Ruth Boerger, Roxbury, CT
Printing: Thomson-Shore, Dexter, MI

ISBN 0-937013-40-4

©Copyright 1991 by Martine Bellen

for Mei-mei Berssenbrugge
and Bradford Morrow

I

But in masquerade there is nothing to be known; she's all *terra incognita...*
  John Dryden, *Marriage á la Mode*

CISTERN

forced forward toward space displaced from reason—a well—the hollow with exposure over and over subverts sequence to a stranger and other order outside the unnarratable.

or if knowingly cut the gnomon nomad measures locked light preceding its likeness without that unbridgeable gap where fishes pass echo not simply

can any knowledge be so young or too old or withdraw itself or water that is temporarily removed till night appears ready, but what sort of coming is it if informed we have choice but denied the right to turn back the dead

forgettable as thought

Insoluble body was her past and time takes all tomorrow if you toc it up to the clockmaster who screws a fence or the negative gate of separation

stake heart through oak track

Disaster never appears but hides in people doing its bidding and the sufferer has a liking for hot tears and mortal movement toward a new era with relations mutilated, too cut to run past and don't say don't go in; the greatest place of hiding might be suicide, a see-saw is-was act of disappearing where no one can return to squeal an answer, any one makes the question possible:

or if Oedipus's swells were knowingly cut the gnomon nomad circuitously measures light locked into shape preceding set course he follows after its likeness hence the fact that nothing is without a doubt, that unbridgeable gap where fishes pass through gas like echo in order not simply to destroy but approach repose.

any one makes the question speakable since body he writes of as being a misleading link to danger or can be disposed in a dram and the answer won't lack madness which is thought's guardian when wakeful,

save waves of sleep which watch over tacit surfeit in drift, and knowing becomes lighter at the hour edges of our parallelogram

other not posited opposite site and part of the content's in too dark.

For one hundred years she slept under sea with closed sense and in that deep the crashing blood against bone transpired night was never longer belonging to her and how she fathomed in.

can sculpt new curves of thought but composition continues

After stars blow out the sky a smothering blanket of eight sights where no one knows an indiscretion in self torments torrents and overflows

loamy sediment and music make love made late in her life even ever after or look not at fallen mortals but the twins who fell from the well immemorial asked favors where smaller folk closer to the hardened dwell and imagine gravity the center of a secret harbored within the larger cartel that can't be strayed from the mass of themselves, "When did I start?" "Where do I awaken?"

CAMISADO

Across the bridge a basilisk waits for breath and your past with the weight of what you live—a complete description moves inside a universe indefinite because of finite matters. And stars unbounded by direction. No one must note the secret, though it may be known there is text stored in the solar nervous system which we will never enter. The knowledge is possible but not its possession:

A castle deep not of this time we sought for what the dead take with them with a rigor that frightens; eyelike spot on ocelot looking nothing toward. We are drawn to the lazy pagan majesty where once a mortal error breaks the crawlspace lock all falls into the cellar. What wails lie open in this game with inner moves?

Turbulence expands universe, and black groves suck the donjon dry of ineffable drift. We enter the missing sin through water though Iris, inseparable seer, cannot dissociate wind from air on any one layer. Hold on to the rim of this linear sea.

Spheres of seen perish when washed by fire; a chorus composed of our female friends seeks the things obscene. And after his face you are no longer, but make too much of leaving the cellular by star. Being detaches itself from inversion. At bottom it may collapse onto the beach at your skull, a circumstance of mortality where every wave breaks and rejoins. What you were ends frozen across the horizon.

CERULEAN NOWHERE

How she functions in the face one's eyes accustomed to producing source and wings shut slightly somewhat severed from limits in extended body and limbs; the heavens their shoulders upheld upon her, how she once said all we do affects all that is or the other, but it's never a solution just temporary countenance overlaying conspicuous duplicity that inspires insomnia and some say it many times slowly, "The reality is minuscule and diminishing."

nowhere but enlarged by rivers and softened with scarfs cannot be encompassed in a single space but is a span of many with embodied desire obliterated–, is made of flesh, dies, then reestablishes and contrives to escape itself

If souls awaken while bodies sleep then theirs are strangers, stranger are their bodies encased by the cipher or charms linked to similitude loom, peripatetic are they in a liquid world window

from forms of Morpheus or weakened spot in magnet causes woman to know closet members even after the house is outdoors and all materials used to separate winds undone strand dead and converted

cerulean terror tight

She wore it cinched or inviolable eschewing embodiment for so many worlds furnished as to deprive one of that most useful time seen on his brow, on her chin, a two way clown, both in and up.

When she thinks the things that were she recognizes him at once though he wears masks that denature the way he appears to relinquish control over direction of his narrative or theirs as one eventually does within imaginary architecture, the walls off his palace or wall it off and build a neatly symmetrical relationship between two legitimate couples, moon and earth as mutually moons a duplicated play when one is new

but the appearance of things not as they are in fact

mumming misrule, a name and its echo, or desiring to be less specific she guises as the domino when divesting and asks which is mine?, where is my missive? How time has broken we still suffer it and light controlled by computer revealed in the only possible way as sailors saw the coming current through lighthouse mirror but still weren't saved, what enters all knowledge, to enter it into a machine or to enter it the ship entangled in his fur he is lost in her cream and she in this colorization their knowledge foisted upon earth.

In the brilliant rule of a bridal underworld, she is kissed first by all man then wrapped in sheet, white by light paint, sky, her youth revitalized each dawn to tell of vanity but also asphyxia as she drowns the sea in mucous, her waters draining into something grander that she supposes she must be a part or germinating principle. The study of past turns in tomes entitled collectivization and liquidation or lethal water easily forgotten where phantasms are taken by vapors; they may require a degree of heat to support their lives and consume them away, as she.

Na_2SO_4

One always wins,

as a symbol on no one's no world outside herself in him, peculiarly resembling what he has learned, the blind stain by which it is possible to know her through him so becomes between two verities seldom seen but during eclipse as his nearness to the sun being ever distant, the gun a ghost or child of him

shade over a lamp as movement assumes outlines of inner shapes so she can see her delimiting moon, ancient lighthouse, mirror to the sun or sun's thighs, a fixed mist sits

                                          is minuscule and dimini

she en . sh

DIAPHANOUS

Through

Women

In visible

bars placed in the vein, insouciant and hands working pots or plants of air-rain, light looking through him to his gesture with too much forced upon her, she tries to see

Less

To see

Something

If added length's desired, stretch firmly into the night below where she lives meaning before observed or moongathering on serving

Lifts life with her foot

up a stair and holds it

In her head. Stars shine

because all of us know too much of the beyond or that we needn't wait longer than six days for molten to find its fissure for whatever doesn't belong to this week will be led out from her and one need only eat what is sacred to understand and endure tenderness drinks deep
....

through it she saw the farthest built walls of the universe the longest time ago and frogs, cattle disease, darkness, disparate plagues, forced the closing of her pupils into her past when she danced vagrant on the desert before an image imposed over space vanished, but that is expected because her people are through a telescope and she must bring all water with her

cooked in time, the egg drops, as does its vessel

Filling tunnels   a lover who can't move space
Pure purple   discovered by staring
Spill   into the other and letting

the same white seen on another side of his gesture when she feels differently

he said "Drink me." (It is not immediately clear

She is aware he is thinking she is not too clever but he is not aware she is aware so maybe, she thinks, she is more clever than he though neither can understand why cathedrals are made to resemble the insides of sex and neither is aware of this feeling that becomes each

They enter

Together

Tongue on
glue

ILINX

"Circumscribe your sex" is a thought of without or a maze suggests the primacy of an un-hidden bitch as such with respect to him in hiding where he immediately ate the horizon meat vermilion at the labile chamber. Terra incognita—posterior to possibility and Dread goddess owns what is swept off earth

what is sweet

Fancies hung on line in thin, forgive me for who I am, I be her insufficiency adrift if truth is above error and abstraction precedes the deepest depression, too passive still to suffer as no language controls which wish— ?

prolongs the hour senselessly and each word spoken permits new misunderstandings in the guise of creating. Perhaps her mystery is he searches for her boundaries eaten; he is what he can believe when he sleeps with thought most lost in day or she vanishes into his own type of dark, febrile and promenading down night's esplanade, exposed to flame explode, and she sees his other with dreadlocks of an involved design while sorrow like time runs out of frame.

What takes place all at once prolongs the hour senselessly and each word spoken permits new misunderstandings through the guise of creating by boundaries eroded; he is what he can believe as he sleeps more lost in day or she vanishes into his type of dark, nested febrile and lost in thought—promenading down an esplanade, while she sees his other with dreadlocks of an involved design and sorrow like time runs out of frame.

seen from outside her womb, we recognize passed from seed

Take the ear strangely while waters flower inconsistent and meet at their playful advance, not knowing no part matters more any in involved change.

incising that which longer is the serpent in or roiling new mind dressed over the other robbed of trouble or truth blown

in her innards hear

She awaits her prolongation at the gap of one landmark near waterway returning him to where he sleeps in unshareable burden. She lapse at his disposal to disarticulate through proliferation and who ever finished fishing at the utmost lost contact tho no one can answer why; us thus once and for all, one for one believes too much when it has been proven there is nothing to it but a surplus of knowledge and thus turns its back back, so occupied by space that the shape of the unearthed

is it possible she dedicated herself to reclaiming the singular sound as though one person could be above or exist without all others

On his knee he claimed: Once there was an Evil undressed that haunted in chamber a maid black and regal who connected no star or hour so the court ministers threatened to undo her neck from her torso if there be falsities and she looked not at the sky but into holes the size for light to slit through and this was what she was and never would pray to what could be seen for what could be seen   ?

Stones blown in cave's mouth with the infinite Furies extracting loss but never spoken of or it's too noisy inside to hear so too the refusal to respond by letter on letter paper that offers space, humanized to the outer side of orbs.

deem ocean a sea with stem for seeking thee forsaken as eye has secrecy in scenes yet not

Who was it that arranged the chairs so she by crystal blue the backdrop earth around holding her in indirection, a new lover able to please by gardening that which he could give—sapphire petals and necklace what jealousies exist by being all things to others as the indifferent passes her the wind she heads it off and catches electric.

She cannot expose, just seduce, albeit resistance of nudity where mind breaks matter and all ill is undeterminably strange with unfinished separations. A sister so racked by loss the unexchangeable results issue from the opening components that make.

VOYEUR/VOYAGER (A NARRATIVE)

It started out of love and now an ocean rays or expectations on it to arrive come to me to be not rearranged transmuted and reformed borne of the crest and pass beyond material Nature to the quality of airiness, alas be gone, Dear Dark, into the sky, enfold, enlarge, where it goes nobody knows

wasn't windy very foggy—a drop cloth for paint—and crash over the group of adjacent nights steam and forms frozen air, how they with calls recall separating what can be seen while up is always open though nothing is found but too too much.

Walking south on Carmine Street

some birds migrate two thousand miles and salmon travel to reach home but the sheep never leave their hoofs wanting

As an aphasiac she knows there might be a relationship between these sounds pieced together a completed puzzle picture and with it a world brought to light; the error or fault is her, a receptacle tunnel where waves might enter, lose direction and therefore

So if she were to walk by walls at the latitude of +544 and N17 who would not understand stones carried up the sides of mountains if mountains have sides for divisions and the difficulty of smaller numbers going into the larger, or even worse, does the inside or outside fit into the other or how can it? The simple logic of picturing one's fingers no longer works and everything one doesn't know one should look up there in your hands sometimes you can pretend by changing words or counting out of sight.

The subway stops in the Orkneys, London, Paris Puerto Rico; just close your eyes, you'll arrive

an in door inside the doors, well-lit showers with light, each corner known in that nothing appears hidden, all genitalia out front from dark—gay! She paces the room. Traces each step with another and places the sole down with the utmost confidence that the floor will be there when she reaches it, for it, and that it will hold her, have her, though something frightening is revealed in that which is habitual. The truest trust transforms into anxiety when you realize it has no reason to be what it pretends or maybe there are factors involved you know nothing about, perhaps a peripheral character who is pulling strings, can act erratically and the bodily awareness of another world brings to mind that there can exist that which you can't see and therefore might be in corners you thought you knew so well that you became a traveler of only them, a traveler of fearlessness you called yourself in these particular walls now no longer belonging to all you acquire a private chamber where you cannot close your eyes, the room tightens and expands what one sees like the breath in your belly crushed and you wear a mask of a lawyer, nurse, mason, and below that is a sphincter, gulf abyss, a grotto where all that was familiar and hospitable becomes a hospital, hostile. Madness enters, reshapes, rehaps; perhaps god's adversary was his tool that he flung upon the tiles of Earth. It is not fear of death but of loving her born to that loss with which you were familiar in a moor before the punishment of having your navel cut out and nailed to the wound and your intestines wound round and round around

Their souls would have wound up presiding in their temples of fresh meat flesh regardless if they were red skinned or black or simply skinned and a dew damp drew desire forth to faceless recesses. What they wanted most or what felt most true to them was running as one group, holding chairs well above their shoulders, screaming toward the brick wall with a painted image of Prince, his mouth also opened. It was an act of united inner wills imprinted, no fear, humiliation or individual weakness of personality could have gotten in the way when they were one, no one. The Land of Wands. The land of Wandering, only wash if it's affixed. The inimitable donne innominate in a garden, headless their breasts are said to see for them and they *are* the Land of Nod.

one who held her tension in her stomach where no one can see but rumbling away and pains she feels full from allow her to remember that not just organs are alive inside but also there is matter and the ghost that was and wasn't there resided, re-sided her a home with icicles on eave renewing wing

She leaves her home in morning believing she will not get caught on the outside or direction that she walks in order to come to the Marketplace. Rows of surplus under colored canopies and prayer rugs; roguish calls and swearing in the air airing out the need to sell and buy each day another story's lost and caught between their clothes and hearts of pomegranates, ancient red flesh with beads get giddy on and spit into the earth; plums, frost licked purple-black or green; raspberries; strawberries; starr fruit; kiwi; kumquat; potatoes soiled tan and gritty, she leaves these fruits in market and merchants call her name to taste to touch to spend all time she's earned to open them and close herself to change the shape of who to how to what

SEA MASK

a green face incarnadine sea. If he saw it through her mouth-eye full fathom five nothing could fade passing through a ding-dong hell hourly

She shuts yes but weakness is weeping grief pressed or her cheeks pressing her away from the infinite pay she owes love without awareness refined.

Even her violence is a demarcation for inertia. She lifts up his genitals. The cat. Salty. And she acknowledges there are two tongues—one she understands and the other that understands her within which exists past and present, though the plaintiff's exhaustion wields obsession without flood or selfhood or she says I want to nothing but it is not only during dying that god casts and holds one to sink, or day

Through the cemetery gate, shrubs separate the inside work earth where one now rests or body lies from the land or lad where bodies walk, where we are hidden in her belly for her to keep us warm and use as fuel, the question faced

the inside walk earth around where it rests it lays cut from body and holy

a possibility for her to zoom through. So vulnerable to hands, feet, when a fly.

One sees only a compilation of what has been, for all porous material, when windows are left behind and closed, changes meaning and leaves so much out or how many hours can one want before the want changes? into what?

Sirens masque with sea sound pressing ear to order hear her white and then they disappear into bubbles

On august seas—unsuccessful ghost that makes mask of those who wade inside, so her joy has more to do with the way it dwells on high and all relationships reflect who authors death on what; what is in a family but the sharing of disease? It is not the other who breathes life into her but without him she believes only giants could create such walls from fingers, though maybe there are cracks for slippage as walking is difficult these days and she feels fine near the cat who needs no one but loves

Choice is mythical and each time we choose to glide sky is brought to ground though dispossessed from an origin which must be necessary for movement away or to a point not yet spotted on yeasty waves, but must one always haul the hoard along where one can find nothing of oneself alone, ordained

Each says some of so much she can't hear pressed against the black heart under every thought that divests when color falls to earth not spring with flowering wind that wills her back to when they first touched down and felt herself afloat. He said there is multitudinous space that can't be founded and with this she was in perfect agreement.

at the masquerade all senses masked by liquid flushing travesty or run out of time or space or space-time or run there were no women conquistadors but troubadours yes in voice at least there is a mask to see but hear not what is in what's held back and wants to run out the end to flesh destroy the both and for forty days it came down upon her a honeymoon ctenocyst clear and pressed a sack that broke hearing so there was no chance

II

...[Moon creatures] may hide in the deep shade behind their excavated mounds and, in keeping with the sun's motion, shift about inside, clinging to the shadows. They have, as it were, a sort of underground city.

    Johannes Kepler, *Kepler's Conversations with Galileo's Sidereal Messenger*

THE STILL-BOUND

Lay thee down the dwarf from under earth, a moon may climb the darkest side and we will reach in memory as chasms can. Divvied up this fear annihilates shadows before what later will exist. We fail to dream but only what's believed.

She looks not through the clerestory window though sees something going out her eye while stain changes vision and she reacts with involuntary mental movements. Meaning extracted as light is caught between living and its look. She thinks farther than the traveling show, an imagining that soon as a new soul appears the last one is gaseous. And imagination: like genii from an inkwell it cannot be drawn. Even there, walls break the earth into corners.

She could not live someway outside herself in a room she lets for sleep and to hold her in, but she is mostly aware of the terrorism, not how she found her way lying. There is a place of bodily grief. As long as it exists mind cannot destruct though it has to be as complicated as what is left under. If she detaches emotion from the external cause one mistake contains more truth than another, the kind of analogies that exist between them. Errors played backwards eradicate the previous from the new and an object of regret ceases to be a passion when becoming an idea. It cannot recollect anything without obliterating the distinction between factual and conceptual sensations. Imagine what would happen if the thought aroused emotion and the game kept something of itself? She might feel movement in common with the inward ear, sound off body; sometimes one can only believe where music leaves. It falls down from pain and the assignment of place. At the ocean she was warned not to break what others made.

HOLE

Most households have a cave in back under the child or a building complex with beauty parlors which women enter midwinter and when they return for the evening their hair smells of sea and their flesh of fresh salt. The understory of a forest we slice open between words and memory, the gesture of mouths shutting, eyes panning lies live parallel, well within ourselves.

In her apartment, there is an empty space. She stands above the plot left for her in earth looking down at her story. She knows what will happen. Between her self and her soul there is a place. Outer space and inner. He jokes about losing vegetables in her. And fruit trees. There is a garden, she disappears into it; where no shadows exist she forgets.

To open the earth costs, reaching depths of glaciation—twenty thousand year old crystals hidden in under-air no body has touched. The last impressions pressed up against her, stored in earth like a memory candle. She knows rational destruction, an eruption, her thoughts projected against specter across a cross of night. It's her mind she's not familiar with, yet.

By its nature it is not in print, she tries to remember it on her tongue. The concept circle has nothing to do with language, neither do switches, inverted image of her mirror memory stored safely from children. Even the child in her self will never reach that high, carrying a piggyback shadow or voluntary prisoner. She crosses a body, of water, the warder of the brain. Will she find its absence in time? Shutting out the space where woods come from, burning to clear room, I can testify to its melt.

It exists as color forms. We know where it came from, the subaqueous, right between the surface. When she exits from love her eyes create light projected onto skins, the way you spot death, catching sight of flight across the eyes. There were no flowers to pick so she picked bones to offer up to space; she tends to build inward, must be abided but she can always construct or dismantle, or a man can do it for her; join all lines—a verticality never attained.

As soon as one settles on a planet. Action. We catch up to our cells carrying a portable kit of images, useful maps. She looks inside but doesn't know where the solution is, on a blackboard perhaps. Walking into past mind, the battle over her memory. Who wins? Who keeps its most important moments? She gets custody of the child, the man of the house and car. He can drive away to strange parts. It's light in this hole. Each sun rising is that much different or she is that much different after each night. Scream. It goes back to a wish.

STORM

"As a child I lived in a small town. We always have a full moon. Every night after dinner, my friend and I gathered round the backyard to play. My favorite game was to play with my shadow. We used to punch the shadow against the wall and set fire to it. Even though I was told my shadow would come to haunt me, I still did it. I did it to find out if my shadow had more strength than me."

Edelyne Gelin

Since the Big Boom we are but one sentence, an internal idea without pause, always a keeper of gaze and one for time, an eye in fantasy or we wouldn't dream what is most fearsome: the presentiment that there must be a realm which assumes a self-contained sister system and only one mirror image for each property, while I myself have found we are independent of one another; this I know as the object I am, and without truth-argument in common, we can be infinite and never cross the other's line, ignoring all words that aren't needed to assist our existence; yet if a union does occur, our multiplying thoughts aren't a casual nexus but imperatives in the midnight air with orris arising out from brick pouring open shadows we wrestle with corrected vision in space between story and its penumbra.

Un

Her shadow she kept in seclusion to see without detail what seemed to make her more an object than a need of faith and hold heart to her ear. She saw herself blind, allowing fantasy the only eye that existed or there would be no sight so she said let it be that you shall see, and it saw her, and she would not have to be the camera of herself. Mostly in dreams she was disturbed for her eyes were shut and still she took notice—breast, vagina. Fog across the bathroom woman after storm; there is a reason in science why first she sees nothing, then slowly the cloud dissipates to find parts bare before her and others gone. To be blinded means not to have eyes hurt but to see something wrongly or to think you see one thing while an object from another dimension is before you. This she knows from her showers and can see as surely as God has sisters secluded with words while He basks in light and steam.

She ate clay tablets of Black Christ under streets to understand possession is occupation of land. Of thirsty roots the size of spreading loins and singing trees, the beetles come to take the song, to own their time, to see the storm approaching which wills no shadow.

During the total eclipse she became impregnated with spirit and struggled with that demon brought inside by storm; thus, the idea of quality perceived is determined from motion or again as an arc of points, but not borrowed toward moon. The form invoked involved in words exists as it is reflected subjectively—a girl and therefore in nature, though not necessarily contrary to His hypothesis of the thought He once was. They clasp and twirl gaining speed and loss and no one falls; some fail because the corm has more strength than we can conceive.

PLACES PEOPLE DARE NOT ENTER

If mind marrow is severed; if the holy body
Cannot move what happens in outward motion
Thought; if the whole
Cannot be present at any most moment;
If the intellect develops in dangerous places
Then the body will not be
Recollected after.

Mind determined motion fills the universe with shapes, movement follows the possibility of form and thought is outward. She is thinking its area. The brain is built by the will to feel it cannot reach such dimensions, though the farthest star starts her limit by one room by two. Even if the idea of duration has no end it is affected by her saying it will be cold tomorrow, and rainy.

This walk wills soil and its vibrations that accompany her to the places she desires because she must; what was she is cut from the present-never. The land of her birth will in all ways be her now, the collateral circumstance of each situation she could not know at her brisance.

Where sorrows sever
From morrow, thought exists
That does not form from her;
The expulsion of her atoms and new vessels
Her body builds for involuntary temblor
Or that which follows through which something else conceived
Succeeds. Mostly their cause determines purpose.

Ancient thought may begin with an object, flame with cerebral compulsion of males compared to females marring sense organs. Eternity exists outside them, though he grants no promise of exile to the panorama where they burn each year and smells wrought the heart. At bottom she is born into mind where brain is dampened and the body cannot move as she wins ground or plants roots in dreams that know no idea of her.

SKY FRAMES

Spires, geodesic domes, mirror-labyrinth, tractors, an Ethiopian lion, plastic human brain. She has an impression of it stepping out her head. "Journey 28, January: what water wants to weep me sleeping sorrow after sorrow."

How can she count an hour's past? if first must pass the half, then half again, never-reaching end. Whether water seems wonderful or not she is prone to divide extended substance. Molecular structures millions enlarged, sky frames, transistors. Hallucinations all in time, there is no telling stone from space.

Number attained from the addition of thoughts. If one divides into many, are there more, or a fraction? Small moves never calculated, wedged between the tragedy of nonexistent individuals violating extinction. In principle it cannot occur though the idea may exist. Nature of notions. What wants to see me in the middle? The line between viscous and excessive.

Our most vicious part in unique architecture. Better to have one's fling in a small rooming house than an unidentified past. Time of removal is encroaching. Her pubic hairs dissolve after seventy divided by heart. It's a train line. Horizon. "Journey 29, January: Why can't I obey, even if I hear no command? I have gone back and hailed her out of death where I do not belong. Allowed to enter for a thought, they tied it to steel."

Rapt in present. In Tiin. Commitments to past emotions or just memory of what was anger. Regna. After I understood she was writing in mirror, the act grew quite charming really, clandestine.

At noon she'd sneak from her room, order up hallucinations by serial. I spied her through (plot) (woods), glassed in egac. She musicked off the boles. Ocean of emotions full, motion of moon, of light scales. Of scare. Full. "I am between my rememory. Each time it becomes more difficult. I touch Satan and know it is Satan. Though I am aware it may be satin. It may be you who can't be held like a body, not in mind."

The organic form as impotence establishes movement out matter. Adam, a highly concentrated image of Mother. Mada. It was her whole fish she could not sever like reach from body in spot, one: Can death and birth no longer function out of order? For all who looked down glass, did not object to world lifting.

ABSOLUTELY

How far have you gone this evening or passed between remembrance other? The vacillation is ours, pure, not land outside the sin fenced in.

What makes it space, a trace-wound wound around hide so far back that she carries her body through it with the notion there is always something behind: A memory, a confused constellation, a white substance of which the heart cannot take the purity and cannot be conceived out of this world where her deepest errors steep suspended on gossip and even if she stays awake, shift in placement occurs when air's gone astray or the spirit's sent off without flesh; for there is nothing so fearsome as no image and no thing to recognize we near.

In weather she is timid since last light finds a way down to set free from above and turns away tidings. Always an absolute span as it curls out of her, withdraws, while snow accumulates, must mist over a moment of loss that is an image, not meaning, and deflection of passion is depicted by drowned river or heaving sea. If she were a bridge drawn between two spans of spirit she'd be walked over.

Field of identity sustained, still part of the entire surface, a kind of thought that walks through her into a snowy field; she is all but a ghost, and he can talk freely about matters outside her. The more she fades into the woods the sharper her outline and dimmer her concupiscent flesh. The words spoken about home automatically enclose in the roof or framed by windows while she is climbing a tree and can only be sought on branches pointing to what isn't known. Into the recess she freezes needles, needs breath no longer and footfalls of small animals replace her but she accepts this as the part of nature she'll never be a part of. Acts can be played in absence and the world is that much changed.

When done in a glow there might be an estuary that lay ahead.

Safe inside magma, the blind daughter and her brother with translucent skin feel no whether or which, just wet light lost to the clouds. With a telescope she brings it into sight of escape and who the devil also compels, pointing to the line from his heart and his private parts in the brain where we buried him so he could begin in a lone direction, already canonized for admitting the most souls, flesh-shed and supine. Each one masked so she could recognize them in herselves—their motion and sensation of sound in encamped concentration.

You try to remember where you came from but with each step there is less trace to your past.

After he steps on her wrist, disturbing her intravascular volume, ocean closes up, though he can't cry in her high concentration of salt and peace. Anywhere is the same and motion the distance between everywhere he is not. Nor does the distinction between earthly and celestial bodies become obsolete with the acceptance of flight and the possibility that what he sees or where he is could be other; the alteration of something into else makes self-evident identity is not a relationship between objects. She could not be seen before he saw her, though nothing allows us to conclude he sees by eye.

, and how this body relates to where it is or the bodies around it.

She is the wall of water from where she sees. Before her—a window with solunar ice, behind her is devotion. Before her are bare trees, behind her the world starts from what she imagines. She's not sure they are eyes though wishes he were present to know the snow casting shadow melts into crests.

Her land has this sin in it but not that one though the sky overarches and turns it around as she holds herself out into morning and names its possibility toward back thinking where she exists already as a stranger lurking to loom wonder in suspense.

When sketching, she takes the pose of her studies to understand their feats, falls to her knees to feel the flame around him, and in charcoal, draws the ashes to her fingers, scarred as she unlearns years. It is already simpler. She can turn all situations into pictures on paper and question the possibility with the irruption of speech. If she conceives a body as its movement then something else exists that depends on her life and greater, more complex bodies in mission. She can't think of his name without changing shape. There is much outside the facts that concentrate into questions through three incarnations and many miles of motion. Across the way a friend is wiping with a photo of Ceausescu's blood.

She can answer to where spirits and ideas have an absolute exterior existence, where space with trimmings out of reach absolve her, but even if what she sees is not correct there is sense in that we always conceive another who is greater yet never satisfied.

If you turn to follow your markings the tread has all but been erased,

After falling out of the forest he forgets all secrets, forfeits cards and earnings. He has memories of feelings but one cannot hand over a promise of the sun and its arrival with mauve strokes, the color of liver without delineation and the inside of her. An amassing of images, of magic, passes away and right or wrong fade from a bruise. One need only proximate experience; death flounders around skeletons, is attracted to light like the buzzing. When the dutch door opens you'll be able to answer most questions.

before you a trace of what night might come to

Without warning her home became dangerous, tears from other parts of the train she traveled through and observation intersected into infinity with written women; it is the nature of scattered memory; it is the privilege of reentering renaissance and finding herself in his pockets of flesh; it is important to analyze how this particular feeling is composed and then dissociate all persons and things so it is only her own. The spectacle is doubly visible if her footprints are carried away and pulled into her pieces as she bursts from east to west. The gaze disappears and they diminish.

and is trampled upon by an imprint that was once yours.

Looking through a window one thing is sought and another seen, so what she sees when she looks at him has two heads, little to do with looking at the window and this she is aware of but it's right before her on the other side. And she knows part of it is a secret and can't even be saved and she has to be, and she is in him breaking laughter with the danger of mixing aspects from a real realm with what exists in the other, so that some characteristics seem so plausible she passes over them while some bring her straight back into parts of herself that couldn't be recognized around the eyes nor does it affect the body, but only the feelings made possible by the knowledge of things invisible. Movement influences passion and property too so the snow falling everywhere makes him an ocean away though why the eyes bulge in space where there is little nothing to see has not been explicated, yet she believes that it has to do with the theory she could ride light to his face and know him by reflection only. The soul has to be made desirable

It was once yours.

DECEPTION

What could empty the universe of its human content? Would it take place in a moment or last?

In the beginning the sun burned out her eye and her womb was a human hum. I carried her in my pocket one hundred and fifty days while oceans completed intuition, imagination. Crayfish appeared out the pond. Her last half hour of memory frozen in the early stages of our enfoldment.

There is an altar in her back. I placed it to feel her bend a stretch of space between cranium and moon. She closes her eyes to be in her head, wraps arms around torso to be in the body. Crosses legs and hearts. Meaning shifts out of her. She reaches around her mind for a scar, treats the place that hurts. Someone switches questions inside so she sees in a different light what entered. Meantime, monsters, monsters more resemble man, guard cathedrals she prays respect in dark only she can see. It's a shape like the pain she screams from. She might tell herself she knows in her bones it will never stop, a feeling that is her in a whisper, a two-way dream characterized by out- and inside intimate.

A situation of rememory escaped as a child and entered during a week. She walked into me, courting death. His blade up against her marked in blood where she didn't exist. When it reached her limits she blinked, when it ruptured the air—no mirage but a seeing in secret the eye under siege—a memory image of her and there's no doubt about it being an independent film of thought with sound, pain, taste in odor coordinates which fry themselves blue. I can smell the contents coming to me; sometimes I don't recognize one and am not surprised.

In a dream she watches herself, knowing the felt through blank face memory images know. She is traveling still, not yet at structures that break without notice. A trace of experience found in the brain, a disregarded cell she haunts.

It's easier for those no longer mobile to pass through the many appearances of memory fading within the face; light substitutes for her person. I chart her at every quarter, and if she misses she strays in sleep. Scream stalks her house. There's a fresh one underside surface, a depth before her where nothing is hidden. She lies inside expecting a message, but receives a signal when meaning's caught, pouring out black, or is it lemon?

Who happens out the mammal room, next the throat, then the attic where it's warm and many sounds congregate. A whole course of thought before her mind in flesh, so she can get out of this, won't have to exist through words chosen to create her, confining her in creation. Maybe she'll remember right before death what's frightening, when the organization of our company changes light, at the point of vanish. Though there is no love at this moment, her hunger makes her aware.

III

The *Earth* is surrounded with a thin vaporous Air, call'd its *Atmosphere:* This reaches every where to the Height of about 46 or 47 Miles; and serves to suspend the *Clouds,* furnish us with *Winds* and *Rains,* and serves to the common Purposes of *Breathing*; it is also the Cause of the Morning and Evening *Twilight,* and all the Brightness and Glory of the Sky.

Rev. Mr. Turner, of Magdalen-Hall, Oxford,
A View of the Heavens

SWIMMING OUT A SPIDER'S WEB

Furtively it traverses on air, enabling imitation without proximity while abolishing a distance. Spider weaved the original orb, that of a secret or indicator and addition is a thing of sand; she attempted to transform her movement into vision but it is the spectator who is connected dots, carries past perceptions—man in the moon—till tell we're breath held apart and briefly make contact in frontal foray

perilous is since thrust upon us like birth that we try to imagine never occurred but were chiseled from glasscakes no one could dare eat and are safe. I know this and what I don't say know best, can keep to myself where unceasing and uneasy I sing both parts, that blind spot absorbing all, I only can reveal it with a difficulty and it becomes most meaningful. Cyclops discloses the underscored

why is there is? Of bone? Aberrant or not. The unbroken being wings. He be the web or orb weaves no note

or the clearing is a brambles withheld from within. Innumerable particularities of slaves, of selves, staves: exist to enter and why return the flour? Was a servant only to the surface

was a servant on the surface. You explore my thirst without reply within me and fail cruelly. It cannot be colder than winter, and anyway, if one were perfect one would know oneself perfectly. This world formed without us and now we are the star. You from suppressing shadow surpassed and doubt within an unknown made of the same as that which is known and even if I understood I wouldn't know more than. Nor are there shadows we imagine as threat all because formation of fires in history and our discovery in its features to reckon with the incidence of you can do it wrong, candescence. A laugh, hips hoot to find a way into your matter like at the movies when a force rips off her flesh and the audience close eyes, can't bear to see what transgresses imaginings and all possible: a,b,c,d. There are reasons we sleep pressed down

ships in space patterned after a navigation of e negative, pattering hail against the utmost border, can be unknown yet knowable, can be unknowable by nature. We think meaning is hidden there, in river's veins. In you. You think if we connect your dots

Renderer of larva consecrated to continuity or servility, a non-discursive inwardness barters almost identical desires to the visible extreme of existence. Origin is a modern thought yet we keep searching for it in the past, try to discover what enables all events to take place the way they do and the child says a recognizable sound but it isn't a word until she wants from it—name, profession, manners with the sun too bright to see before and after we're gone or a fly haunted by wing cannot succeed without each order or even the other resembles accumulation streaming in, in pure volume.

FUSION :

...or the starling who flew into a windshield ending simple night and vocal, opal ocean

dropped

or skin breaking

as she shouts out the storm in air from their rain

such a star

down

does not describe a figurative space

sea-room and even harmony

toll:

Need for fear and loss is different than to feel afraid and lost.

2

If all the ghosts were locked in their lovemaking more would come out of them and they would see the matter in parts usually separated but brought together by unforeseen means or circumstance. She screams into sheep and feels his shivering in the language Belief that resembles life but doesn't exist in it, all the time suspecting a fleck of obsidian between her.

She can no longer wish anyone to be everything to the point of death, the voluptuous shame and shape that she becomes.

it is the child who is ghost

how its body was an errant, concordant echo, hollow and ensouled

3

Rays from a point fall on corresponding localities and are conveyed to a single visual center, producing the impression of one:

spitting image

Being in her everything begin again. This is your world she joined, solo for sound blown and fiat. Soil will be it!

4

There is no rule you never lose illusion or its counterpart, the found echo in shape spotted around invariant intervals that testify to absence. Time is compressed or expanded to fit her need for belief in certain things and endless for the still scream airing area under its ring. If you could subtract her knowledge, her background, would she still be the she and could you say you knew her if she were not where her voice was or in a forest? Begging is a form of speech too and refusal to communicate the most hostile means of divesting

The ghost surmised what the hunter was after but trapped in the haunt
      if conclusion escapes

5

the melting of crystal in its water.

PRUNELLA AND SAINT LENARD

Laughter starts at the base of the spine and rises through the sex cunt bit before it swims up solar plexus or other brain cloud can be pregnant seen wet. She holds it, her nose, practices death while fucking, so the two sisters will meet, the way they do in our bodies.

The sweetest dream of you
She had   You
Were the music
Of her   You were
The sweetest dream she had

but after entering where do you roam? if exists a labyrinth or room on the other shadowed side a door alone, if there a window, whether or not she is heat or rays, whether there is leaving

Writing is reductive like making sauce, like a genie in a bottle but when you read me let me live on your lips, in the air outside of which nothing makes sense outside of you

the M14 [Cloisters to Penn Stat.] takes 1 hr & 1/2, 1/4 of which is spent riding along the width of the Pk allowing ample time 4   1   2

I'm not sure what the new piece will be or where it will go, though I think I know its title and there are characters, clowns, several, and hermetic writing on the hem of a maiden's skirt that can only be seen by a magus who won't be written in.

veering along the park it interacts with the north side traveling east much as the imprints circumscribing margins of medieval manuscripts pun off text and therefore comment on what was not explicitly rendered but implied not by the configuration of letters but sounds that inhabited the inner sanctum of the scribe not the one who commanded the word.

Pelican kills its young, but receives them three days later with her own blood and the sacrifice letting means bringing her nearer to surrender is rendering to the above pours herself into them or up them, her he swims to make more of love, out of life, wanting/

Introduce me Master into the cellar, dark, into yours, like a bride in church, white against the wood of God, stellar speed pass seed see me it is almost opposed and over

And the Virgin said unto Beatrix "I have stood in your vagina for 15 years and now that you've returned take over yourself as no one knows of your departure"

One can eat the tripe but not the stripe of gold around its crown

Eat me she said, Drink me, I am your sister, your side

Fornicator, gen *fornix*, hence low underground vault, hence cf: *fornax*, steamy or furnace from the bowels of water buffalo, as a provider of fuel

Prunella beside the tower a black nun bowed, bower empty, passing through he can't make us say whatever he wants.

Prunella wants to divest, legs speared, spewed little silty grape seeds or Doomsday Book taken up by writers who need words whether sounded or configured, taken up by force, ravished, taken by force

What are these things, like two balloons, passing beyond the body

it's a bad bad habit she has she has of being elliptikal beginning and never finishing the numerous translations of her remains impressed without expression but seeks beyond the confines of the sentence as of course can occur in spoken language where the confines between bodies are overcome with equal amounts of milk and heat or allowing meaning to arise from a lengthier context the scene is not limited to straight space.

He was not only (meaning he was) the patron saint of prisoners (judgment

kathodos, descent or down way therefore negative or female, emerging from the vacuum tube through outside space modified by small window.

It was the introduction of the window that distinguished Saint Philipp Lenard's rays and tubes from the others and as he was the patron saint of prisoners he understood the necessity for that most simple architectural structure

The space laid around it commented on what could be seen or worked as a course determining factors for destiny around her laid life way low for to be who she was with him or who they are as conjoined manuscript in that this could not be spoken between the two (hermetic, and therefore) and also it is that interplay which causes them never to exist in the same space, or adjacent space, as the foliage and espaliered pear trees grow in knots, so too the space of the margin and enclosed cloister garth in intricate design or intrinsic, most secret inner, hence private belonging to one's essential being one with nature, continually interchanging roles, where one at times is the border and the other the wheel, repeat, design as it travels from eye

" 'to be on the margin' means you haven't any color, perhaps a mere mark of a pencil and not affecting the text," was said to the woman of color (Prunella), "perhaps not even noted by the reader, as in earlier text-times, it was other furniture found within but doors between each passage unbolted or official world secreted aslant bolt forward an indication of murder executed by one inside or familial"

when the moon was emptied or weather broken

(insert story of St. Lenard and how it came about that he was sainted, complete with accurate descriptions of miracles attributed to him and our savior, the boy dog)

his key grating in the lock after having cemented his fingers to hers and balm emulsifying their joints, milky seed spread just not enough alone to rub in how alone she could be as she mopped up where he had been between her earth and hour haunted

a window transparent yet locked and a maiden peering out *through* a hole (St. Lenard & Prunella)

She kept in the shade as was her delight when crossing the apartment whose curtain dropped before the tresses let down there is a missing heart, now more protected, pronounced.

VOYEUR/VOYAGER

1

Down the permissive path where icicles eccles appear, she happened upon a time ago beside the walls, what does she build within? A stone fell or ghyll? Or soft washed marsh

Her church over the buried while under-feet unite all rushbearing and less yellow light is taxed, our lefe left in furze or a scorpion entering erected, she makes list of all line, the rules between and where she goes at night after kissing; there is no fire in the morning.

2

Since the time he's gone out of her frequency, one sees what one knows how and shuts oneself off, fades into scenes, her face beams bright with butterflies, not as efficient pollinators as hummingbirds though temporality increases ratings as does the length of her hair. Even when caught in broth she finds release through a grounded pea pressed her till top opens her heart and out flew flies a door ajar into party part of her formed balls and home to a room of cards.

is she fell a map of here

3

To pass the time one's most intimate aspects taken out of surroundings: if the object is a person and normally functions in one setting when possessed in an alien the possessor knows her as his familiar environs onto the flesh and she is seared by soft yellow from the vase she is placed next to and the lamp rays sideswipe; or if the object is a thing and becomes a part, it forfeits the utilitarian purpose, grows greater because of what stands beside it and also, for the same reason, is diminished and exists as a pattern or unit of the design to show. Why does one feel the need to collect and have rare important/

4

some—prefer answers from
—voices—, hers hooked—by the bay,
a bit—deeper each—Time
she recognized the—Sound—waves as
her own till—denied she—could
object and yes say yes I—see
and am—seen, the—closest
thing in a closed—closet
—. One senses there—is something
under what—she—wore. But it is—
belief of Being—tied gagged
hoodwinked) hooked and no—Power to
stop say out ouch stay—off of
my life—of my life or dream,—
see, I see my hands—I can
draw you away or—change
directions new. —Notice
it's a female tied to—a staff.—
Something about—wateriness
of her—passage—I see a passion

5

a plumb line woven into the cut interrupts a meaning invention or creation or one that inspired the surface and she became part of the blanket or cloud between the vaults and prairies she resided

Into the design she walked

INVISIBILITY

1

A messianic liquid remembers you and yours as one imagines taking oneself for night or off to it:

as one imagines dipping into a pool

electrons enclosing nothing but swim in a storm of charge and none of the particles which constitute your being are seen. Even after the beating becomes a part of you, movement arrests time, till it no longer moves and you cross

a street, moan for no apparent reason and think, What is a monster? Draw it in its appropriate color,

she dips into the pool, water deflects light, radiates an aura around her, an aurora, so she is almost, almost an angel.

2

When you dive into another's body sometimes you are erect from him, as with the earth when your feet join its head.

3

With no way to fight the charge

Brought upon her, pain

Links to portions of her body—her

Oceanic throat or the coiled mountain

Roots down her neck. No longer

Can she hold the enormity of this

Nature; it means little If not linked to life.

4

or adoration bores says god in his black night gown that he moves through like an undone cloud, perpetually summoned forward

5

Frankenstein and his creation raptures you, switching hands from right to wrong while she's found partially on the east side eaten and then there's some on the north pole lost.

...During violence I asked G that all the world be denied a voice as lovely as mine, fully aware I was hideous progeny; my wound extended farther out the house, past the pool, than can be imagined, depriving us the possibility of seeing him or ourselves, or the Germans who drowned in a teaspoon of salt mines. I could say mind hatred has to do with humiliation, but that would be invisible. We haven't those parts to exist.

STALEMATE

Practically speaking, he asks, where do we move from here?

as she thinks into his face no one will recognize lines on paper draw resemblance to that which isn't

he asked   from there

....

but also to hear understanding translated in the hollow of another's mouth and after all she knew even the inside of each cheek, that much she knew in him—

as instinct hallows the book which is itself spirit or he the room she waded in,

in need of direction or certainty

who defeated or what drafted with each letter unable and if it did who ever would wonder under the night below upon (us) them mean I anyway?

discretion separating salamanders unscorched by sublimated laments according to why carries accurately through her secret visitors in ear dwells

, what has been spilled

so long,

Has been

....

Even at our most rational, ruled by first thought that wasn't transcribed but became our warrior or she worried over its absence, the lack of sense was true because she feared most how that too became a her of her a part as she a he stood back to storm with no authority to speak of clear the sea, area vast and ungraspable where power lies, paralyzed in impassive passion motion StoP. Can't you fucken be alone without these always watching around you? She ventures to allow herself found there, but closes the face as one does a past if you can put your fingers through it you know _____ and they are both ghosts, (when he speaks of possession the flesh fit in) moaning into words all so close they almost sound—

we al[ms most were, but may b[e go]

ech[o on form ro]om no moor no mor[e go]

....

for moments at least and suspicious of anyone who knows liquid so well as to tolerate Proteus mirroring blindness, cannot imagine what shape she lived on or how the cat lapped; is that you whom she came _____ if it weren't for _____ when mind the mind changed, grew itself things and flew to where choice immersed occasion once on a time in the guise of girl's puberty or state of perpetual readiness as it was and is insatiably the distance necessary to sacrifice that which divides divine between the st. where you come from and have you any?

CODA

bellicose veins tattooed on the blue belly of your once most secret place, single linger still and linear

mouthflies hovering over when the dying stops there are uncontrollable degrees of closeness

are we attached or involved?

deep down the manhole a hum or sung to someone in the sea
hear
seep

Potes & Poets Press, Inc.
181 Edgemont Avenue
Elmwood, CT 06110

POTES AND POETS PRESS PUBLICATIONS

Mickal And, Book 7, *Samsara Congeries*
Bruce Andrews, *Excommunicate*
Bruce Andrews, *Executive Summary*
Bruce Andrews, *from Shut Up*
Todd Baron, *Dark as a hat*
Dennis Barone, *The World / The Possibility*
Dennis Barone, *Forms / Froms*
Dennis Barone, *The Book of discoveries*
Lee Bartlett, *Red Scare*
Beau Beausoleil, *in case / this way two things fall*
Steve Benson, *Reverse Order*
Steve Benson, *Two Works Based on Performance*
Brita Bergland, *form is bidden*
Charles Bernstein, *Amblyopia*
Charles Bernstein, *Conversation with Henry Hills*
Julia Blumenreich, *Parallelism*
John Byrum, *Cells*
O. Cadiot / C. Bernstein, *Red, Green & Black*
Abigail Child, *A Motive for Mayhem*
A. Clarke / R. Sheppard, eds., *Floating Capital*
Norman Cole, *Metamorphopsia*
Clark Coolidge, *The Symphony*
Cid Corman, *Essay on Poetry*
Cid Corman, *Root Song*
Beverly Dahlen, *A Reading (11-17)*
Tina Darragh, *a(gain)2st the odds*
Tina Darragh, *Exposed Faces*
Alan Davies, *a an av es*
Alan Davies, *Mnemonotechnics*
Alan Davies, *Riot Now*
Jean Day, *From No Springs Trail*
Ray DiPalma, *The Jukebox of Memnon*
Ray DiPalma, *New Poems*
Ray DiPalma, *14 Poems from Metropolitan Corridor*
Rachel Blau DuPlessis, *Drafts #8 and #9*
Rachel Blau DuPlessis, *Tabula Rosa*
Johanna Drucker, *from Bookscape*
Theodore Enslin, *Case Book*
Theodore Enslin, *Meditations on Varied Grounds*
Theodore Enslin, *September's Bonfire*
Norman Fischer, *The Devices*
Steven Forth, *Calls This*
Peter Ganick, *Met Honest Stanzas*
Peter Ganick, *Rectangular Morning Poem*
Peter Ganick, *Two Space Six*

Robert Grenier, *What I Believe*
Carla Harryman, *Vice*
Carla Harryman, *The Words*
Susan Howe, *Federalist 10*
Janet Hunter, *in the absence of alphabets*
P. Inman, *backbite*
P. Inman, *Think of One*
P. Inman, *waver*
Andrew Levy, *Reading Places, Reading Times*
Steve MacCaffery, *from Theory of Sediment*
Jackson Mac Low, *Prose & Verse from the Early 80's*
Jackson Mac Low, *Twenties (8-25)*
Barbara Moraff, *Learning to Move*
Laura Moriarty, *the goddess*
Melanie Neilson, *Civil Noir*
Janette Orr, *The Balcony of Escape*
Jena Osman, *Ellerby's Observatory*
Gil Ott, *Public Domain*
Maureen Owen, *Imaginary Income*
Rochelle Owens, *from Luca*
Larry Price, *Work in Progress*
Keith Rahmings, *Printouts*
Dan Raphael, *The Matter What Is*
Dan Raphael, *Oops Gotta Go*
Dan Raphael, *Zone du Jour*
Stephen Ratcliffe, *Sonnets*
Joan Retallack, *Western Civ Cont'd*
Maria Richard, *Secodary Image / Whisper Omega*
Susan Roberts, *cherries in the afternoon*
Susan Roberts, *dab / a calling in*
Kit Robinson, *The Champagne of Concrete*
Kit Robinson, *Up early*
Leslie Scalapino, *clarinet part I heard*
Leslie Scalapino, *How Phenomena Appear to Unfold*
Laurie Schneider, *Pieces of Two*
Spencer Selby, *Accident Potential*
Gail Sher, *w/*
James Sherry, *Lazy Sonnets*
Ron Silliman, *B A R T*
Ron Silliman, *Lit*
Ron Silliman, *from Paradise*
Pete Spence, *Almanak*
Pete Spence, *Elaborate at the Outline*
Diane Ward, *Being Another / Locating in the World*
Diane Ward, *Crossing*
Craig Watson, *The Asks*
Barret Watten, *from Two Recent Works*
Hannah Weiner, *Nijole's House*